A
TALE
OF HER

A TALE OF HER

By

Maanarak of Grey

Look mom! I'm a kintsukuroi pottery, mending myself after being broken. Not only by love...but by the cracks created in childhood, the chips in adolescence, and shatters they inevitably came to be in adulthood.

Table of Contents

FOREWORD

Funny thing, the human experience. It is essentially a series of events—some great, some unfortunate—and when they are unfortunate, we seek a villain outside of ourselves to blame, be it the moon or the rain. But perhaps it's the name of the game. Perhaps we all have good and bad things happen to us, because it's meant to. Everything that goes up must come down. Affirmations for positivity are lovely, and necessary. However, what are they without the recognition of all the negatives that caused your prayers for the opposite? What is the light in this world without recognition of the darkness? What is the Yang without its Yin or the Yin without its Yang?

I've always been a writer at heart, and lately I've written a lot of poems while processing these events of my human experience. I've decided to share these poems, along with the story that led me to write them. Within these stories, I seek to recognize the good, the bad, and everything in between. For it is my opinion that they all form us, and they all have their place in this world. I hope that by sharing these stories, I can inspire you to have peace with the events in your life. I hope I inspire you to bask in your unique essence and take back your power.

The events you are about to read have certainly shaped me, and the woman I am, or rather, the woman that I am becoming. This is her tale; these are our stories.

HER DEATH

My story of recent human experience starts here: in a relationship coming to its inevitable end. During this period, tensions were high between my partner and I. Even though there was always some form of tension present, this last year, it felt as if every other word out of my partner's mouth was criticism of anything and everything that made up my being. The list was long. The way I dressed was too plain. The way I acted in public was too reserved. My body was not tight enough and I had cellulite. My friends were few, and they weren't always hanging around my house. I didn't kiss nor fuck like her previous lovers. I didn't want to dance, as instructed, and I didn't twerk to her rhythm.

And there I stood, day in and day out, accepting all the disapproval, all the attacks on my person, until I started thinking there was truly something wrong with me. While I am in no way claiming to be perfect, it was fucked up to have convinced myself that those harsh words were out of love. But I did—I had put myself under a spell of wanting to achieve perfection, just to be accepted by the one I love. Until one day, the spell was broken, and I set myself free. Sure, I was heartbroken, but I could finally see the wreckage that I came to be. I don't know how to explain the intense sensation of pain I felt after the break up. It was as if every insult I took in was shots fired at me, but I was too numb to feel them before.

"Years of Russian roulette with words like bullets, now feels like voluntarily standing in front of a firing squad convincing myself each shot was with love."

After the break up, I found comfort in someone else's arms. I didn't want to be in my small studio apartment, with the one who had just become my ex-girlfriend. My friend invited me over so we could be sad together. To be honest, the moment I walked in, I knew something was going to happen. We laid there embracing each other, comforting each other after having our hearts broken. On the second day of my visit, the embrace became increasingly more intense. As I stared at his lips, I started to feel the urge to kiss him. Then, he suddenly asked if I wanted to try kissing. Of course I did, so we did. We felt a chemistry neither of us was ready for. To me, it felt electric, like a merging of our energies.

Yet there I was, conflicted. I had just come out of a long-term relationship. *Should this be happening?* I asked myself. Regardless of my inner conflict, I let it happen, because it felt right, even though the timing felt wrong. It felt like something between us was bound to happen at some point in my life. But why then? Why when I felt completely broken and void of life? I wished it had happened when I felt stronger—fuller of confidence. Maybe I believe it would have had a different ending if the circumstances were different. Maybe I would have been more willing to share parts of myself he has yet to know.

But now I will never know if that would have made a difference. I do love the thought of it having worked out in an alternative universe. It gives me peace, but it also makes me wonder. Why is it important to me that some version of us did end up loving each other in the same way? Perhaps it's the potential I felt. Or perhaps, it's hard to believe that I'm the only one that felt this connection.

"Pandora's box opened with a kiss shared amongst two grieving souls. And for a moment, I think we both felt whole."

In the weeks to pass, he made it clear that he was not looking for something serious, at least not with me. I was upset when he first said this, but I agreed to it anyway, because part of me wanted whatever part of him he was willing to give. Every time our bodies met, I was left with his energy. It stayed there for days, sometimes weeks. This caused me a lot of confusion, since we were friends before any of this. Unexpectedly, it made me want to behave differently towards him. I held this urge back with all I had. *That's not what he wants from you,* I reminded myself. I felt that I was merely another girl on his long list of conquests—not girlfriend material in his eyes.

Some reasons were obvious, and admittedly, some of the things I wanted were irrational. I was not in the right state of mind. For example, I wanted a baby, perhaps to spite my ex-girlfriend because she found me disgusting after learning I was having unprotected sex. Of course, he didn't want that; it seemed he just wanted to fuck as many pussies as possible. Some reasons were less known, at least by me, because I never cared to ask why he's not into girls like me. What is a girl like me? Whatever the case, I was only fit for physical pleasure.

And what hurts is not that he didn't want me as more than that; it's that this version of us that could be still resides somewhere in my head, as I simultaneously long for the friendship we once had. To add insult to injury, the friendship we once had is, in my mind, the perfect foundation for a lasting relationship. But maybe I'm delusional, and the friendship was not what I originally thought it was.

"My love deepened like
trenches in the sea with
each convergence between
you and me, tectonic
shifting the plates of my
soul. Oh, how I miss you
swimming in my ocean,
but I can't bear the
loss of you as you jump
between different bodies
of water. It makes me
boil like a kettle, as if
I don't possess enough
liquid to replenish your
vessel."

One Sunday morning, my feelings became too much to bear. I decided to confess my feelings, knowing he did not feel the same. I had already felt it before, when we spoke of things like children and settling down. But at this point, I said, 'fuck it.' It was time to speak my truth, and so I did. I sent him a long message. In hindsight, he must have felt blindsided, because I kept all of this in for months. During our conversation, he expressed hope that we could simply close Pandora's box and perhaps in the future become just friends again. I proceeded to bare my soul, and it was then that he understood that our intentions were not the same.

I'm not sure if our intentions will never be the same, but then how is one supposed to keep some sort of friendship going, when two individuals have completely different experiences of love for each other? Difficult, some might say; impossible, might say others. I say it's worth a try, because how can I love and care about someone so much and not even know if he is doing alright?

I have no idea how long it will hold, how much of it my heart can take, but I feel that I must try, even though it will likely never be the same again. How can it be? That ship has sailed. The box once opened, unleashed something that can't be contained again. All we can do is reopen it and see what else is left. What can help rebuild a friendship?

"I've learned to comfort
my heart with gentle
petting of my chest.
Sounds of applause for
it surviving all I've put
it through by wanting
people who are unable to
return the song it sings
for them."

HER REBIRTH

After these heartbreaks, I found myself wondering how this happened twice in a row. Perhaps it was me and the future I imagined having with them. The alternative universe inside my mind kept me imprisoned in pain—the pain of them not seeing the potential I saw. It takes two to tango, you see.

I realized that I needed to stop wishing for things with people who don't want the same with me. While I did love them both in my own way, I couldn't help but wonder if this strong attraction came from them being emotionally unavailable with father issues, which is ironically the issue I had with my own father growing up. Whatever the case, I shouldn't be wasting my imagination on fairy tales and happily never afters. Though there is nothing wrong with being a hopeless romantic, I should invest my energy elsewhere.

So, I write, and I create. In creating, I reclaim my energy. In doing this, I go on adventures and discover new things. It allows me to let go of things I never thought I could. It offers a strange kind of comfort—at least I can control what I want to do with my time and my creativity outside of the daily adult obligations we all have. It doesn't matter that lovers, who were previously just friends, become just friends again. Maybe one day, they become the friends we randomly visit. And maybe accepting that a lover's heat has cooled becomes part of the memories we now share.

"You gave me comfort in my darkest days, and between us a potentially undying love was overthrown. R.I.P. the fondness I had once shown. Release the love that I now hold, as I grieve for a lover that has gone cold."

The following months, I spent a lot of time thinking about what happened—flashbacks, overthinking, etc. Sometimes, it made me feel like a fool; I felt like an idiot for allowing all that to happen to me. In those moments, I laughed and vowed to never allow it to happen again, but this was the wicked kind of laugh—that of a scorned woman about to release her wrath. Like the late musician Prince said in his song titled Fury: "Ain't no fury like a woman scorned." Yeah, I was angry, but luckily, I am mostly vengeful in my imagination.

I know there are things I have no control over, but I could control how much of my power I gave away to others. For so long, I allowed others to determine my worth, my mental state, and my faith. As a result, I felt stuck and sucked dry of all the life force inside me. I'm slowly recovering now, but it is one step forward, two steps back. I am progressing slowly, but progressing nonetheless. Every day I use these affirmations that are so popular nowadays.

Moreover, I try to live healthy while still allowing myself my humanity, for I may make mistakes. I may not be perfect, but I get up and I am 100% me every day. That's the only thing I can control. And some days, even that is not true, when I am at the mercy of biological cycles. Regardless, all the decisions I make each week, hormonal or not, have been my own. I remember distinctly choosing my actions with the intention of letting go and stepping into the next phase of my life. I'm ready, so done with begging people to see me, to want me back, etc. I don't want to repeat these energetic cycles, with relationships of any kind, be it lovers, friends, or otherwise.

"I feel drained,
emotionally chained
to things out of my
control.
I feel it's time to
energetically let go."

Being a person with the urge to understand everything at its core and armed with months of overthinking, I started to piece together elements of past traumatic experiences with my current behavioral patterns. With each realization, more pieces of the puzzle became available. For example, one night, I dreamed about why I was such a people pleaser. I love dreams—they always reveal things to me. This dream revealed childhood moments where my "no" was not good enough, not loud enough—moments when my "no" triggered anger in others. No wonder I freeze whenever I feel this energy from others. Every time I showed my back bone in the past, people got terrified, and did all they could to bring me back to the docile version of myself they were used to. The version they were comfortable with; the one that shuts up and does as she was told; the one that puts others' wishes on a pedestal.

That was easier for them, I assume—more manageable and less confrontational. When I woke up from this particular dream, I was done with being nice. The thought of how many times I said yes, when all I really wanted was to say no or be left the fuck alone, enraged me. It led me to take immediate action to reassert myself. I realized I had a long way to go to completely reprogram this behavior, but this was a start—another stepping stone in the right direction. I was set on holding my ground, showing my teeth, and letting no one walk over me.

"A new wave of magnetic energy
pulls in to cleanse the stagnant field
turned foul. A new rave, from now
on this wolf growls."

I recognize that much of how I currently react to situations has to do with my childhood. Growing up, I always felt like an outcast, even back home. I felt it when I was amongst family, friends, acquaintances, and even classmates. I always hated fakeness. I valued honesty, in every sense of the word. The fakeness people dished out when in social settings made my stomach churn. This is why I developed a disdain for inauthenticity and putting up a face for society. Though I still tried to fit in at times, I always failed. I become awkward in a bad way when I try to fit in. It's as if my body rejects this imposter and starts to twitch, as if to say, "Help! All I want is to be myself, but this environment does not feel safe enough for me to do so." I'm afraid of being rejected, but perhaps I have been rejecting myself in an attempt to make others more comfortable around me. And then there is a vicious cycle of trying to balance my comfort against the comfort of others. In light of recent events, I've come to realize that people may reject me either way. I cannot control that, as I've said before. All I can do is not reject myself. All I can do is unveil the woman I'm destined to be—the woman I am in my wildest dreams. Thus, I don't care to put on a mask, unless I'm invited to a Venetian dance.

"The feeling of not belonging is constant, reinforced by guilt for not being able to play along. The confusion in my voice while questioning: "should I play along?"

It's truelife is but a stage and we are but actors. Does that mean we all have the same role or that we all perform to our own script? The confusion in my voice while whispering: "perhaps I should play along."

The feeling of not belonging is constant. Reinforced by the assurance that I can only play my role...the confidence of the voice increases, I know I could never play along."

This woman I am in my wildest dreams is on the other side of a wall—a wall that I am chipping away at. I am healing from all the shit that makes up this wall. I am missing the beautiful nature of a small Caribbean island. I want to swim so badly, at the salty beaches with sparkly sand. In my culture, it is known that salt water holds healing properties, and that's what I long for. I long for those waters that could help me carry my pain and remove my sorrows. They can help weaken the wall between me and the woman I want to be. Essentially, I want to leave my sorrows in the Atlantic Ocean and borrow from its mighty force to regenerate myself, and then for the sun to shine a light on the new and improved me. But my current reality is different—I'm having to regenerate myself with nothing but memories of how it feels to submerge in those salty waters. Maybe next year, I will make it back home. By then, much of the wall should be down. Then, the water will hit differently—I'm sure of it. My gut says it will feel like a baptism, and that woman will be ready—visible behind what's left of that wall. The water will wash away the last bits, and it will cleanse my soul. And at the end, all that will remain is her.

I'm not trying to say that it will magically remove all my problems. I am saying I will be reborn as this woman that continuously thrives despite it all—a woman that is better equipped to handle this world of marionettes.

"Lately I've been hallucinating
While standing underneath the hot
showers. I must be calibrating,
recalculating my worth.
My skin longs for the sun,
My soul longs for salt water.
I close my eyes, I wonder.
In these Caribbean blues,
I wander".

In between healing, introspection, and self-criticism, I found myself accepting my good, bad, ugly, and divine. I wander in the grey areas of myself where light meets dark, Yin meets Yang, where they form a team offering me balance in return. What a sight to behold if you could live but for a day inside my mind, my many sides gathered at the round table, conspiring to be the best version of myself. I'm so fascinated by this grey zone, so much so that one day I renamed myself: Maanarak of Grey. The first name honors all the first names given to me by my parents. It is composed of pieces thereof. I rearranged it to start with "Maan," which in Dutch means moon. This in turn honors my connection to the moon—the Goddess of dark and light, ruler of my astrological sign.

The last name "of Grey" honors this space that forever fascinates me. Grey, the masterpiece we get by combining black and white. This twilight zone where things are obscured, and ambiguous. This area allows both darkness and lightness to coexist in peace, bringing forth something magical. In a way, it reminds me of my favorite card in the decks of tarot. It makes me feel like a high priestess in my own world, equipped with great ambition and a complete grasp of my emotions, connected to the earth, and its seasons. Sitting between the pillars that represent the duality of nature. Mediating the depths of my reality.

"I find myself amidst a twilight zone, somewhere between my darkness, my light. Unraveling mysteries within, I love myself as is, as could be, as I have always been."
"I find myself amidst a twilight zone, somewhere between my darkness, my light. Unraveling mysteries within, I love myself as is, as could be, as I have always been."

As the high priestess of my world, I uncover my hidden talents and use my intuition and my spiritual insight. I imagine a future version of myself, though she is in some ways still a mystery. All I know is, she is the one where all my hard work reprogramming myself has paid off. What will that look like? Honestly, I'm not sure. What I am sure of is that it all started with me loving myself more with each passing day. I took all the love that got rejected and poured it into myself.

Right now, that means I continue to heal, and pursue a path that makes my heart sing. It means that every day I am braver, and dare to be ruder. I set boundaries with others, yet I'm kinder to myself. It involves me allowing myself to speak my mind, to express myself fully. As I grow older and wiser, I will continue to unravel mysteries within myself. It's an ongoing process—I believe that as long as we live and breathe, we'll grow, and we'll learn.

I wish I could say to the woman I am in my wildest dream, that I became her today—some perfect equilibrium between my darkness and light. But somehow, I am already her, and I was always her. I just kept her in the dark for some time, in a corner deprived of light. So perhaps, her tale is in the unveiling, in the freeing of her shackles. Her tale lies in the marriage of the compartmentalized parts of myself.

"The phoenix once again rises, having been suppressed and burned to ash. An otherwise dark moon in a balancing act, reflecting flares the sun possessed. Finally, I can fully shine bright, as my name suggests."

HER MANIFESTO

I have so much love to give. I will be the first recipient of my love.

I value others' opinions and perspectives. They do not dictate my life.

I enjoy making people feel comfortable. It will no longer be at the expense of my own comfort.

I want to be heard. I will speak louder and clearer.

I want to be seen. I will not hide myself.

I accept myself fully. I will no longer reject any part of myself.

I have great intuition. I will honor it.

I give energy where needed. I always call it back to me.

I value self-growth. I remain open to learning.

I am human. I will be patient with myself.

I am healing. I am– proud to have come this far.

I set boundaries. I will respect them.

I value myself. I am enough.

www.ingramcontent.com/pod-product-compliance
Lightning Source LLC
LaVergne TN
LVHW010821200726
843507LV00003B/664